The Shakespeare Collection

TWELFTH NIGHT

RETOLD BY JAN DEAN

Illustrated by Chris Mould

OXFORD
UNIVERSITY PRESS

 *Character list:*

Viola
(disguised as Cesario)

Sebastian
(Viola's brother)

Duke Orsino

Countess Olivia

Sir Toby Belch
(Olivia's uncle)

Andrew Aguecheek
(a friend of Toby's)

Maria
(Olivia's housekeeper)

Malvolio
(Olivia's butler)

Feste
(the storyteller)

As the ship struck the rocks, a dreadful scream echoed through the darkness of the storm. Wood splintered against wood. The deck sloped crazily. Sebastian stumbled through the tangle of fallen rigging, frantically searching for his sister.

"Viola!" he yelled. "Where are you?"

Sudden lightning lit the ship with an eerie blue glow. And there – across the deck – was his twin sister, Viola. Safe! "Thank God," he whispered.

Viola was his double – both in looks and personality. Losing her would be like losing part of himself.

Lightning flashed again and Sebastian saw a huge wave tower over the far side of the deck. It thundered down like a great green wall, battering the ship mercilessly. Then it sucked back, sweeping the deck clear.

"No!" Sebastian screamed. "Viola... *No!*"

Then the great wave struck again and he, too, was swept into the icy sea.

By morning the storm was over. Viola sat on the beach beside the ship's captain. He had saved her from drowning. But what about Sebastian?

"What are his chances?" Viola asked.

"There's always hope," the captain said. "When I last saw him, he was using the wreckage to stay afloat."

Despite the captain's kind words, Viola's eyes glittered with tears. Was Sebastian lying still and white at the bottom of the sea? She could not bear to think about it.

"What country is this?" she asked the captain.

"Illyria."

"Who rules it?"

"Duke Orsino."

"Well," Viola said firmly. "I'm alone now and I must make my way in the world. I'll go to Orsino's Court."

"But, madam, the duke's friends are young men like himself. The only woman he wants is Countess Olivia. You'll find no place in his court."

"Trust me," Viola said.

That night, in a country inn, Viola stood before her mirror. She was tall and slim with a boyish figure. Only her long hair made her look different from her brother. She picked up the scissors and began to cut it off.

Just one trunk of clothes had been saved from the wreck – Sebastian's. Viola put them on. She sat in the chair, an ankle resting on a knee – the way her brother sat. She walked around the room in his shoes, practising a man's walk.

She coughed and cleared her throat – making her voice as deep as possible. Her disguise was complete. All she needed now was a name.

"*Cesario*," she thought. "That'll do. Goodbye, Viola... Hello, Cesario," she said.

She was ready now for Duke Orsino's court.

But Viola was not ready for Orsino himself.

"He's *perfect*," she thought. "Perfect looks, perfect smile, perfect eyes and a perfect personality. He's *wonderful*."

And he liked her at once. Or rather, he liked Cesario. Very soon they were close friends. Poor Viola – she had met the man of her dreams, but was disguised as a man! Could things get any worse?

14

It seemed they could.

"Cesario," Orsino said. "I need your help. Countess Olivia will not see me. Go to her and convince her that I love her. I know you're only a boy, but in some ways you seem so wise. I'm sure you can persuade her."

Countess Olivia was mourning her dead brother. Her uncle, Toby Belch, was sick of it. He enjoyed life and Olivia's mourning was beginning to annoy him.

"All this mooching around gloomy rooms – it's unhealthy," he complained. "Her brother's been dead a year now – it's time she moved on."

Feste, the storyteller, agreed. As Olivia was walking through the great hall with Malvolio, her butler, Feste blocked her way.

Olivia was angry. "Take the fool away!" she snapped.

"Quick!" Feste beckoned the servants. "Didn't you hear Olivia? Take her away!"

Olivia glared. "*You* are the fool, Feste. Not me."

"Madam," he said. "You're sad for your brother."

"Yes."

"I think his soul must be in hell."

"How dare you! His soul is in heaven!"

"Then why are you so sad? Only a fool would mourn for a soul in heaven!" said Feste.

Olivia had to smile. But Malvolio was not amused. "That's downright cheek!" he said.

"Oh, Malvolio, don't be so pompous," Olivia said. "I have everything. Everyone around me does whatever I say, and says whatever I want to hear. Feste is only telling me the truth."

"Excuse me, madam," Maria, the housekeeper, interrupted. "There's a young man to see you – from Orsino."

"Send him away," Olivia ordered.

But the young man would not go.

In the end Olivia gave in, and threw a veil over her head.

Cesario strode into the dark drawing room.
On the sofa sat a veiled figure.

"Are you Countess Olivia? Only, I've worked
hard on this speech and I don't want to waste
it on the wrong woman."

"I'm Olivia."

"Show me your face."

"Did Orsino tell you to see my face?" she
asked. She was sure he hadn't. But because she
liked this young man – who was so direct and
honest – she lifted her veil.

"Ah," Cesario murmured, seeing how beautiful Olivia was. "No wonder Orsino loves you."

"Well I don't love him," Olivia declared.

"If I loved you like Orsino does, I'd *make* you love me back," said Cesario, annoyed that Olivia could not love such a wonderful man as the duke.

"How?"

"I'd never give up trying – I'd camp out by your gates, I'd call your name, I'd write love songs and poems about my broken heart."

Olivia smiled at Cesario. He was very good-looking and he spoke with such passion... She felt swept along by his words – but still she felt nothing for Orsino.

"You're wasting your time," she said. "I don't want Orsino. Tell him: No more messengers. Unless..." she hesitated, "...unless you come back to tell me how he takes it."

Cesario bowed and left.

Cesario had not gone far before Malvolio appeared.

"Sir!" Malvolio called. "Countess Olivia sent me to return this." Between his finger and thumb he gripped a gold ring. He held it at arm's length, as if it were a rotten egg. "She wants no *gifts* from Duke Orsino," he said. "Take it back." And he dropped the ring into Cesario's palm.

Cesario watched him go, and wondered "What ring? I left no ring—"

Then the truth dawned. "Oh, no... Olivia has sent *me* a ring. She has been fooled by my disguise. She loves *me!* Oh, poor lady!"

*T*hat night Olivia dreamed of Cesario, but downstairs in the dining room Toby was wide awake. Feste was with him and so was Andrew Aguecheek – a tall, thin twit of a man with far more money than sense.

"Does your niece, Olivia, really like me?" Andrew asked.

"Absolutely," Toby lied. He was keen to keep Andrew, and his money, in his house.

Andrew gave a soppy grin. "Almost in love with me, is she?"

"A whisker away," Toby hiccuped.

"I'll whisk 'er away," Andrew muttered drunkenly. "You'll put in a good word for me?"

"Leave it to me." Toby tapped the side of his nose.

"Good man," Andrew said and handed Toby a wad of money. "Good man."

" 'Nother drink?" Toby mumbled, greedily grabbing the money and spilling red wine on the table. He giggled. Feste began to sing and Andrew danced like a drunken flamingo.

"*Ssh!*" Maria stuck her head round the door. "Be quiet! You'll wake Malvolio!"

But he was right behind her.

"Are you mad?" he snorted, his nose held high in the air. "Do you know what time it is?"

"You've got a nerve," Toby snapped. "Coming in here, laying down the law." And to show he was not impressed, Toby turned to Maria. "More wine," he said.

Malvolio looked at Toby as if he had crawled from under a stone. "Maria, if you respect Countess Olivia, you'll do no such thing."

Maria stared at Malvolio. Even in his dressing gown and ridiculous night-cap he acted like he owned the place. Maria would never take Malvolio's side against Toby. She got the wine.

"This is an outrage!" Malvolio hissed. "My lady will know of this!" Then he turned on his heel and left.

"Go shake your ears," Maria called after him, "like the donkey you are!"

"How dare Malvolio speak to me like that?" Toby seethed. "I'm Olivia's *uncle*. He's a *servant*!"

"We'll show him," Maria said. "I have a plan..."

The following morning Maria wrote a fake love letter. It was full of lovesick nonsense about a secret love, full of praise for a mystery man. And it was written in handwriting just like Olivia's.

"Are you sure Malvolio will think he's the man Olivia's secretly in love with?" Toby asked.

"He'll fall for it," Maria assured him. "Malvolio's so full of himself! He thinks that everyone who meets him thinks he's wonderful."

Toby and Andrew took the note out into the garden and left it lying on Malvolio's favourite bench.

"He's coming! Hide!" Toby said and they scuttled off behind the hedge.

Malvolio found the note.

"What's this?... Olivia's handwriting... 'To my Secret Love...' " Malvolio tore open the note and read on. " 'I command the man I adore...' " Malvolio gasped, "Why, I am her servant, she may command me! " 'M.O.A.I. has stolen my heart.' " M.O.A.I? Was it code? And then he realized... He looked again at the letter. "M.O.A.I. – those letters are all in my name. She loves *me*!" Eagerly, he read the rest of the letter...

Malvolio's hands were shaking as he put down the letter. "Smile? I will smile until my face cracks! Yellow stockings? Fancy garters? Oh, Olivia! I'll do anything to marry you and be Count Malvolio!"

Behind the hedge, Toby punched the air in triumph. "Yes!" he cried. "He's fallen for it!"

*A*t court, Orsino was pacing the floor.

"Go to Olivia again, Cesario," Orsino said.

"But, sir, she doesn't love you."

"She must!"

"If a woman loved you and you didn't love her back – you'd want her to leave you alone, wouldn't you?"

"It's not the same. She'd soon get over it. Women don't feel things as strongly as men."

"Rubbish!"

Orsino gave Cesario a startled look. "What do you know about it?"

Cesario reddened and mumbled, "I had a sister once. She was in love, but she couldn't tell the man. It broke her heart."

"Did she die?"

Cesario looked away. "I am the only member of my family left alive now."

"And if you fell in love, Cesario? What sort of woman would you love?"

"With eyes like yours, I think... and your colour hair."

Beneath Cesario's manly clothes beat Viola's female heart. She watched Orsino and was more lost than when she had been swept off the sinking ship. She would do anything for this man.

"You're a good friend," Orsino said. "Now hurry to Olivia – win her round!"

*M*alvolio stood before Olivia and smiled. He bared his teeth and curled his lips into a dreadful half-moon grin.

"Is he ill?" Olivia whispered to Maria. Then she noticed his legs – scrawny as an old hen's in bright yellow stockings. "And hideous garters!" she gasped.

He stepped towards her and his grin grew wider and wider. His teeth gleamed like piano keys and his yellow legs almost glowed in the dark.

"He's mad!" Olivia darted a glance at Maria, who nodded in agreement.

"A breakdown," she said. "He's completely mad."

"He needs rest and quiet," Olivia said. "See to it, Maria."

Maria went to the gardeners. "Malvolio's gone mad," she said. "He's dangerous. Find him. Tie him up. Then lock him in the cellar!"

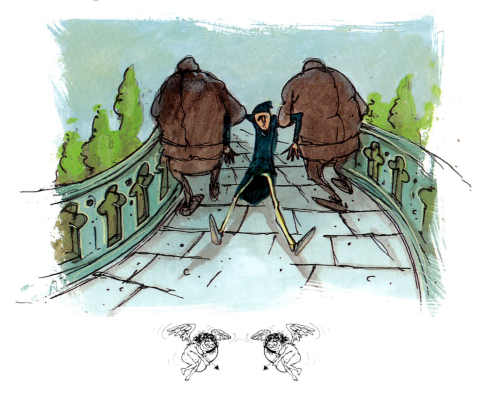

Cesario went into Olivia's drawing room. Things had changed. Light streamed through the open curtains and Olivia was dressed in pink. Her mourning was over.

"Cesario," she said, "what can I do to please you?"

"Love Orsino!"

"But I love you!"

"Then I've had a wasted journey. Goodbye."

"Come back!" Olivia called. But Cesario had gone.

Sebastian had been walking for weeks. After the shipwreck, the terrible storm had washed him ashore far up the coast. Now he would set about making a new life and a new fortune. He rested by the gates of a great house. He noticed the lady of the house walk about the garden with her servants. She was very beautiful in her pink silk dress. Suddenly she caught sight of him. He was the spitting image of Cesario.

"My love!" she cried and ran towards him.
"I will always be your Olivia!" Then she threw
her arms around his neck and kissed him!

Sebastian was stunned. Was this love at
first sight?

"Marry me!" she begged.

She was beautiful. She was rich. A new life
and a new fortune all at once! Why not?

"Yes!" he said.

Hand in hand they hurried to the chapel
where the priest was waiting.

*A*ndrew and Toby watched them go.

"She was supposed to marry me," Andrew complained. "I gave you money to fix it. Piles and piles of money." He glared at Toby suspiciously.

"That rat, Cesario!" Toby said. "He's sneaked Olivia's love away. We'll deal with him. Bring your sword!"

And off they went to lie in wait.

Just then the duke himself arrived to see Olivia. Nervous at meeting so grand a person, Maria rushed off to fetch her mistress.

Minutes later they returned.

"So beautiful..." Orsino murmured, but Olivia ignored him. Cesario was by Orsino's side. She had only just left him at the chapel. How had Cesario got here so quickly?

"What are you doing here?" Olivia asked.

Cesario smiled at the duke and said to Olivia, "I'm here to support Orsino – the person I love best in all the world."

"But you are my husband!" Olivia protested.

"*What?*" Orsino was furious.

Cesario was bewildered. "There must be some mistake. I—"

Suddenly there was a huge commotion. Andrew and Toby raced across the lawn shouting. "Help! Murder!" Andrew had an egg-sized lump on his forehead.

Orsino took charge. "Who did this?"

"Him!" Andrew and Toby pointed at Cesario.

"But—" Cesario's head whirled. This was crazy.

Then another figure sprinted across the lawn.

"I'm sorry about all this, Olivia," Sebastian said, nodding towards Andrew and Toby, "but they jumped me."

Olivia's eyes grew round as saucers. She looked from Sebastian to Cesario and then back again. Two of them! And both so attractive...

"Most wonderful," she sighed.

Now Sebastian and Cesario gazed at each
other.

"Sebastian? Not drowned?"

"Viola? Is it really you?"

Slowly, the amazing truth dawned on
everyone.

Finally Orsino spoke. "Cesario, – I mean,
Viola, I never had a friend I liked so much as
you. And just now you said I was the person
you loved best in all the world... Viola, will you
marry me?"

"Oh yes!" Viola sighed. It was like a miracle.
Her brother was alive and Orsino loved her. She
was so happy she thought she might float away.

*I*n the middle of their celebrations a servant brought in Malvolio. His clothes were dirty and torn from being thrown in the cellar. He was angry and tearful. He looked hard at Olivia.

"Why did you do this to me?" he demanded.

"Me? I didn't—"

Resentfully Malvolio pushed the love-letter into Olivia's hand.

"I didn't write this," she said. "It's a fake."

Malvolio stared bitterly around. Whoever had cooked up this plot to bring him down – he'd make them pay. "I'll be revenged on the whole pack of you!" he hissed. Then, turning his back on them all, he walked away.

"Poor Malvolio!" sighed Olivia.

Orsino looked around. Everyone looked so serious. What could he do to lighten the mood again? It was Twelfth Night – a time to turn the world upside down with wild parties. Suddenly he saw Feste. "A song!" Orsino cried. "Sing, Feste!"

Soon the party was in full swing. Orsino danced with Viola. Olivia danced with Sebastian. Feste's song rang out, and the air was full of music.